Little Eight John

Retold by Joyce Dunbar

Illustrated by Rhian Nest James

Can you believe there was ever such a one,
as bad little, sad little, Little Eight John?

'Don't you go squashing the slugs and snails,' said his mother one day. 'If you do it will bring us bad luck.'

'Oh, I won't go squashing the slugs and snails,' said Little Eight John.

But as soon as his mother wasn't looking . . .
He squished a slug and squashed a snail.

Squish!

Squash!

Squish!

Well . . .

The next day . . .
the milk turned sour.
His baby sister fell
out of her pram.

But Little Eight John just laughed with glee.
He didn't care, oh no, not he!

'Don't you sit backwards on the chair,'
said his mother that same day.
'If you do it will bring us bad luck.'
'Oh, I won't sit backwards
on the chair,' said Little Eight John.

But as soon as his mother wasn't looking Little Eight John sat backwards on every chair he could find.

Well . . .

The next day . . .

the cakes burnt.

The bread wouldn't rise.

But Little Eight John just laughed with glee.
He didn't care. Oh no, not he!

'Don't you go climbing trees on a Sunday,' said his mother on Sunday. 'If you do it will bring us bad luck.'

'Oh, I won't go climbing trees on Sunday,' said Little Eight John.

But as soon as he got away from his mother
he climbed up the tallest tree.

Well . . .

The next day . . .
the dog hurt his tail.
His father's potatoes
turned green.

But Little Eight John just laughed with glee.
He didn't care, oh no, not he!

'Don't you go counting your straight, white teeth,' said his mother soon after.
'If you do, it will bring us bad luck.'

'Oh, I won't go counting my straight, white teeth,' said Little Eight John.

But as soon as he was by himself
he counted his straight white teeth.

He counted his
top teeth.

He counted his
bottom teeth.

He counted backwards and forwards.

Well . . .

The next day . . .

his mother lost her purse.
A robber stole his baby sister's pram.

But Little Eight John just laughed with glee.
He didn't care, oh no, not he!

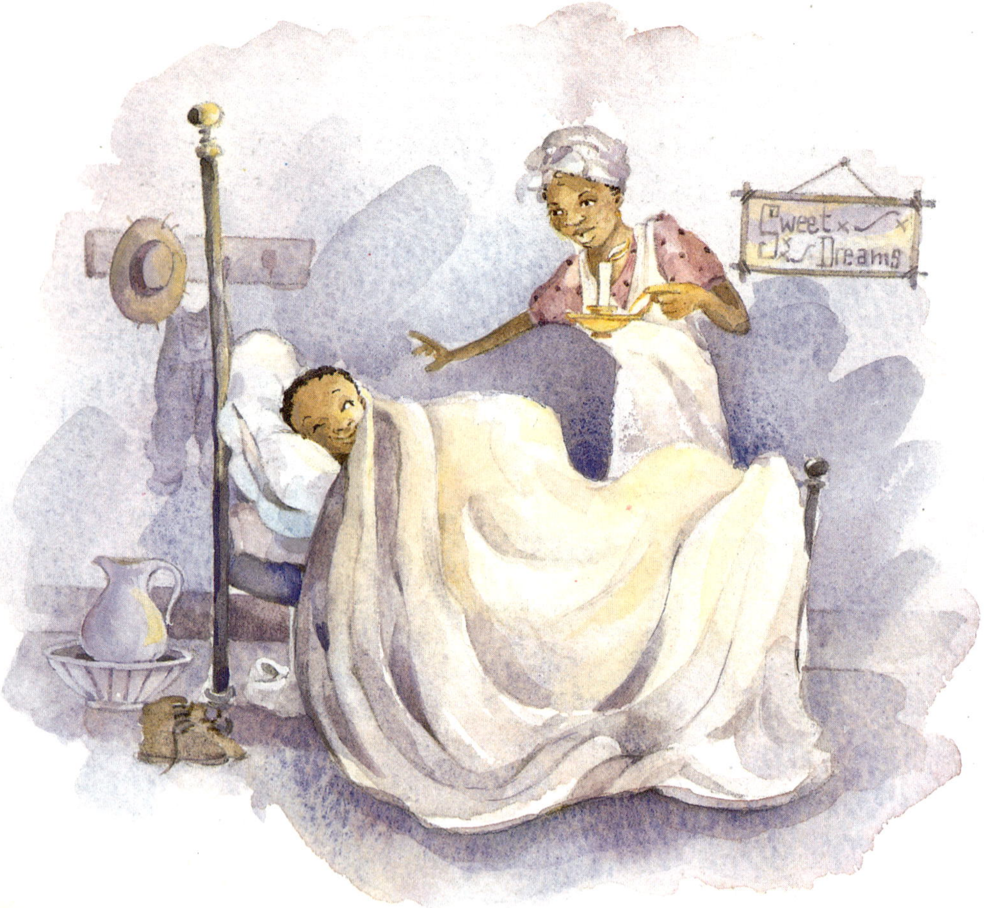

'Don't you sleep with your head at the foot of the bed,' said his mother one dark night. 'Old Raw Head Rattle Bones will come and get you if you do.'

'Oh, I won't sleep with my head at the foot of the bed,' said Little Eight John.

But as soon as he was by himself he lay with his head at the foot of the bed and fell asleep.

Well . . .

That same dark night,
Old Raw Head Rattle Bones came to get him.
In a flicker of candlelight he turned
Little Eight John into a dark spot!

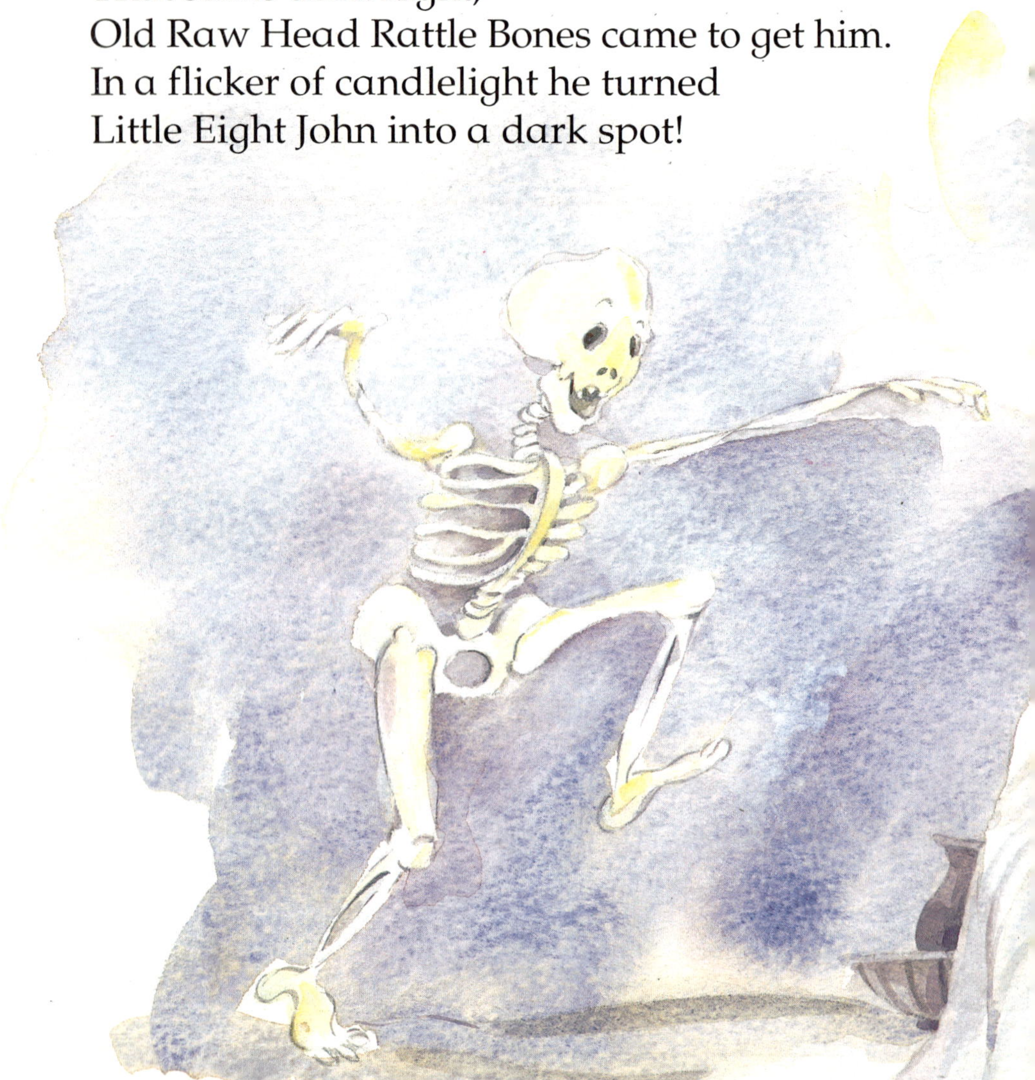

And in the morning . . .

his mother saw the dark spot and was about to wipe it away when it said,
'Mama! Mama! Can't you see?
It's Little Eight John as sorry as can be!'

But his mother didn't hear and she wiped away the dark spot just the same.

Well . . .

I don't believe there was ever such a one
as bad little, sad little, Little Eight John!